THE GREATEST WRESTLERS OF ALL TIME

Gareth Stevens
PUBLISHING

BY KRISTEN RAJCZAK NELSON

Please visit our website, www.garethstevens.com. For a free color catalog of all our high-quality books, call toll free 1-800-542-2595 or fax 1-877-542-2596.

Library of Congress Cataloging-in-Publication Data

Names: Rajczak Nelson, Kristen.
Title: The greatest wrestlers of all time / Kristen Rajczak Nelson.
Description: New York : Gareth Stevens Publishing, 2020. | Series: Greatest of all time: sports stars | Includes glossary and index.
Identifiers: ISBN 9781538247914 (pbk.) | ISBN 9781538247938 (library bound) | ISBN 9781538247921 (6 pack)
Subjects: LCSH: Wrestlers–Statistics–Juvenile literature. | Wrestlers–Rating of–Juvenile literature. | Wrestlers–Biography–Juvenile literature. | Wrestling–Records–Juvenile literature. | Wrestling–History–Juvenile literature.
Classification: LCC GV1195 .R35 2020 | DDC 796.8120922 B–dc23

First Edition

Published in 2020 by
Gareth Stevens Publishing
111 East 14th Street, Suite 349
New York, NY 10003

Copyright © 2020 Gareth Stevens Publishing

Designer: Katelyn E. Reynolds
Editor: Emily Mahoney

Photo credits: Cover, p. 1 CHRISTOF STACHE/AFP/Getty Images; cover, pp. 1–32 (series art) Dmitry Kostrov/Shutterstock.com; cover, pp. 1–32 (series background) rangizzz/Shutterstock.com; p. 5 Jed Jacobsohn/Getty Images Sport; p. 7 Neal Simpson/EMPICS via Getty Images; p. 8 Sergey Ponomarev/For The Washington Post via Getty Images; p. 9 Glenn Cratty/Getty Images Sport; p. 10 Quinn Rooney/Getty Images; p. 13 Olivier Andrivon / Icon Sport via Getty Images; p. 14 Mark Dadswell/Getty Images; p. 16 Bruce Bennett Studios via Getty Images Studios/Getty Images; p. 17 FAYEZ NURELDINE/AFP/Getty Images; p. 19 Olivier Andrivon / Icon Sport via Getty Images; p. 21 Bob Levey/WireImage/Getty Images; p. 22 Steve Azzara/Corbis via Getty Images; p. 23 George Pimentel/WireImage/Getty Images; p. 24 JP Yim/Getty Images; p. 25 Ron Elkman/ Sports Imagery/Getty Images; p. 26 Bettmann/Getty Images; p. 27 Fryderyk Gabowicz/picture alliance via Getty Images; p. 28 Sylvain Lefevre/Getty Images; p. 29 Lukas Schulze/Bongarts/ Getty Images.

Printed in the United States of America

CPSIA compliance information: Batch #CW20GS: For further information contact Gareth Stevens, New York, New York at 1-800-542-2595.

CONTENTS

WORDS IN THE GLOSSARY APPEAR IN **BOLD** TEXT THE FIRST TIME THEY ARE USED IN THE TEXT.

ON THE MAT AND IN THE RING

In 1996, Kurt Angle won an Olympic gold medal for freestyle wrestling. Four years later, he was competing on the grand stage of WrestleMania. Each of these achievements makes Angle one of the greatest wrestlers of all time—in two different kinds of wrestling!

The greatness of amateur wrestlers is measured by matches won, NCAA titles earned, and the glory of national, international, and Olympic medals. A professional wrestler's greatness is measured by their talent in the ring, as well as titles won. Some are also considered great because of the outsized characters they have created and their ability to connect with the audience.

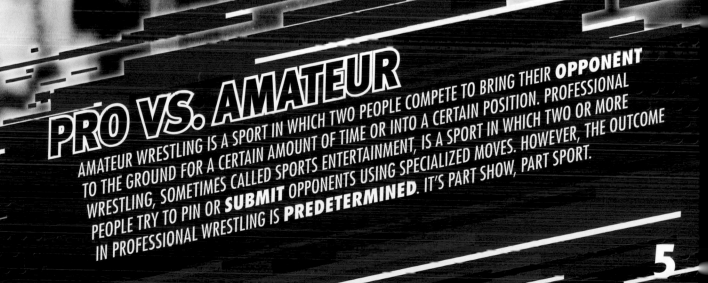

IN ADDITION TO A GOLD MEDAL AT THE 1996 OLYMPICS IN ATLANTA, GEORGIA, ANGLE WAS A CHAMPION IN THE NCAA, OR NATIONAL COLLEGIATE ATHLETIC ASSOCIATION.

PRO VS. AMATEUR

AMATEUR WRESTLING IS A SPORT IN WHICH TWO PEOPLE COMPETE TO BRING THEIR **OPPONENT** TO THE GROUND FOR A CERTAIN AMOUNT OF TIME OR INTO A CERTAIN POSITION. PROFESSIONAL WRESTLING, SOMETIMES CALLED SPORTS ENTERTAINMENT, IS A SPORT IN WHICH TWO OR MORE PEOPLE TRY TO PIN OR **SUBMIT** OPPONENTS USING SPECIALIZED MOVES. HOWEVER, THE OUTCOME IN PROFESSIONAL WRESTLING IS **PREDETERMINED**. IT'S PART SHOW, PART SPORT.

THE SIBERIAN BEAR

Wrestling has been part of the Olympic Games for centuries! That means there are hundreds of medal winners. However, one man stands above the rest, both because of his size and because of his accomplishments. Aleksandr Karelin competed in the heaviest weight class for Greco-Roman wrestling and was known to be extraordinarily strong.

Karelin was the first Greco-Roman wrestler to win three gold medals in the same weight class at the Olympics. He won gold medals in 1988, 1992, and 1996, as well as a silver medal at the 2000 games. Additionally, Karelin won the European Championships 12 times and the World Championships nine times.

THE OLDEST SPORT?

WRESTLING HAS BEEN PART OF THE OLYMPICS SINCE 708 BC! TODAY, THERE ARE TWO TYPES: GRECO-ROMAN AND FREESTYLE. GRECO-ROMAN COMPETITORS USE ONLY THEIR UPPER BODIES AND ARMS. FREESTYLE WRESTLERS CAN USE THEIR LEGS AND MOVE AROUND MORE. THEY CAN PLACE A HOLD BOTH ABOVE AND BELOW THEIR OPPONENT'S WAIST.

ONLY ONE MEDVED

Freestyle wrestler Aleksandr Medved started wrestling when he was 19 and serving in the army of the **Soviet Union**. Though he wrestled as a heavyweight in competition, he was sometimes one of the smaller competitors in his weight class. He made up for size with great **technique** and lightning-fast speed. Medved won his first Olympic gold medal in 1964, pinning Bulgaria's Said Mustafov in 39 seconds! He won two more gold medals, in 1968 and in 1972.

Reports say Medved was offered a lot of money to become a professional wrestler but that he responded: "In America there are many millionaires, but in the USSR there is only one Medved."

IN 2002, FILA, THE GROUP THAT OVERSEES WORLD WRESTLING, AWARDED KARELIN AND MEDVED THE TITLE OF BEST WRESTLERS OF THE CENTURY FOR THEIR TYPES OF THE SPORT. SHOWN HERE, THEY ARE FEATURED IN A WRESTLING HALL OF FAME IN MOSCOW, RUSSIA.

BRUCE BAUMGARTNER (IN RED) COMPETED AS A SUPER HEAVYWEIGHT, WHICH IS THE WEIGHT CLASS WITH THE HEAVIEST WRESTLERS.

A US FIRST

BRUCE BAUMGARTNER WRESTLED FOR INDIANA STATE UNIVERSITY, WINNING 86 OF 87 MATCHES DURING HIS FINAL 2 YEARS THERE. THEN, IN 1984, HE MADE HISTORY AS THE FIRST US WRESTLER TO WIN AN OLYMPIC GOLD MEDAL. BAUMGARTNER WAS KNOWN TO WATCH VIDEOS OF HIMSELF WRESTLING MANY TIMES TO FIGURE OUT HOW TO BECOME BETTER ON THE MAT.

SAORI YOSHIDA

If Karelin and Medved were the best wrestlers of the 20th century, Saori Yoshida of Japan might be the best wrestler of the 21st century. In fact, in 2012, she became the record holder for most world titles won in a row, surpassing Karelin.

Yoshida started wrestling as a young child. By age 20, she was **dominating** international competition in her weight class and earning world titles. She earned her first Olympic gold medal in 2004, the first year women's wrestling was an Olympic sport. She **retired** in 2019, telling ESPN: "I realize I have done everything I can as a wrestler."

YOSHIDA IS THE SPORT OF WRESTLING'S MOST DECORATED ATHLETE—MALE OR FEMALE! AT THE TIME OF HER RETIREMENT IN 2019, YOSHIDA HAD WON 16 GOLD MEDALS BETWEEN WORLD CHAMPIONSHIP WINS AND THE OLYMPICS.

OLYMPIC WRESTLING WEIGHT CLASSES

MEN'S FREESTYLE AND GRECO-ROMAN WRESTLING

- 55 KG (121.2 POUNDS)
- 60 KG (132.2 POUNDS)
- 66 KG (145.5 POUNDS)
- 74 KG (163 POUNDS)
- 84 KG (185 POUNDS)
- 96 KG (211.6 POUNDS)
- 120 KG (264.5 POUNDS)

WOMEN'S WRESTLING

- 48 KG (105.8 POUNDS)
- 55 KG (121.2 POUNDS)
- 58 KG (127.8 POUNDS)
- 63 KG (138.8 POUNDS)
- 72 KG (158.7 POUNDS)

THESE ARE THE WEIGHT CLASSES FOR THE OLYMPICS, THOUGH THERE MAY BE MORE OR FEWER IN OTHER COMPETITIONS. ALL WRESTLERS MUST WEIGH IN BEFORE A MATCH AT OR BELOW THE SET WEIGHT IN THEIR CLASS.

MANY MEDALS

A LOSS AT THE 2016 OLYMPICS ENDED A 206-MATCH WINNING STREAK FOR YOSHIDA. SHE LATER SAID: "I CHERISH EVERY MEDAL I EARNED ... BUT I STOOD ON THE SECOND PLACE ON THE PODIUM IN RIO AND IT TAUGHT ME HOW OTHERS HAD FELT LIKE. SO I THINK THE ONE I WON IN RIO GREW ME THE MOST."

IT'S TRUE!

Before his Olympic gold medal in 1996, Kurt Angle made headlines as a teenager, winning the state championship in Pennsylvania. He won two NCAA Division 1 championships as a heavyweight at Clarion University. In 1995, he won a gold medal at the World Wrestling Championships.

In 2000, Angle successfully moved from one kind of wrestling to another. He made his **debut** in the World Wrestling Federation (now World Wrestling Entertainment, or WWE), shaping his character around his Olympic glory. He even wore his gold medals to the ring! That year, he won the WWF European Championship, WWF Intercontinental Championship, and WWF Heavyweight Championship!

KURT ANGLE HAS BEEN A PROFESSIONAL WRESTLER FOR MORE THAN 20 YEARS, WRESTLING ALL OVER THE WORLD. LIKE MANY PRO WRESTLERS BEFORE AND AFTER HIM, HE CAME TO PRO WRESTLING FROM AMATEUR WRESTLING.

COLLEGE WRESTLING

ANGLE ISN'T THE ONLY PROFESSIONAL WRESTLER SHAPED BY COLLEGE WRESTLING PROGRAMS. WWE SUPERSTAR DOLPH ZIGGLER WAS A CHAMPION AS A WRESTLER AT KENT STATE IN OHIO. WWE CHAMPION AND FORMER UFC (ULTIMATE FIGHTING CHAMPIONSHIP) CHAMPION BROCK LESNAR WON AN NCAA CHAMPIONSHIP AS A HEAVYWEIGHT TOO!

STYLIN' AND PROFILIN'

In 1974, Ric Flair was 26 years old and starting out as a professional wrestler in the Mid-Atlantic territory of the National Wrestling Alliance (NWA). That year, he was in a plane crash that broke his back. Against the odds, Flair was back in the ring 6 months later. After that, he barely left for more than 30 years.

Flair became one of the biggest names in wrestling, known for his skill, incredible blonde hair, and outrageous robes. During the territory era of wrestling, he was one of the most famous heels, taking on other big names in the business: Dusty Rhodes, Ricky Steamboat, and Andre the Giant.

RIC FLAIR

TALK LIKE A
PRO WRESTLER

ANGLE:
THE STORYLINE OF A PROFESSIONAL WRESTLING SHOW

GIMMICK:
THE RECOGNIZABLE OR SPECIAL WAY A PERFORMER TALKS, DRESSES, OR BEHAVES; THEIR CHARACTER

SHOOT:
A MATCH, PROMO, ANGLE, OR FEUD THAT'S REAL AND NOT PLANNED

FEUD:
AN ONGOING DISAGREEMENT OR FIGHT BETWEEN TWO PEOPLE OR GROUPS

SPOT:
A PLANNED MOVE OR SET OF MOVES DONE IN A MATCH

PROMO:
DIALOGUE SPOKEN BY SOMEONE TO FURTHER A STORY OR TELL MORE ABOUT THEIR CHARACTER

KAYFABE:
THE IDEA THAT THE EVENTS AND STORYLINES WITHIN A PROFESSIONAL WRESTLING SHOW ARE REAL

BABYFACE, OR FACE:
A GOOD GUY OR HERO CHARACTER

MARK:
A FAN WATCHING WHO BELIEVES KAYFABE

WORK:
A PLANNED MATCH, PROMO, ANGLE, OR FEUD

HEEL:
A BAD GUY CHARACTER

SELL:
TO REACT TO AN OPPONENT'S MOVES IN A DRAMATIC WAY

COLOR:
BLOOD OR BLEEDING

THE TERRITORIES

BEFORE BIG COMPANIES LIKE THE WWE, RING OF HONOR, OR ALL-ELITE WRESTLING FORMED IN RECENT DECADES, THE WORLD OF PRO WRESTLING WAS BROKEN UP INTO TERRITORIES, OR REGIONS OF THE UNITED STATES. EACH HAD ITS OWN SHOWS, STARS, AND TITLES. SOMETIMES, THEY WOULD EVEN FIGHT EACH OTHER!

THE 8TH WONDER OF THE WORLD

Andre the Giant stood a **massive** 7 feet, 4 inches (2.2 m), and was a larger than life character in the ring. Andre started wrestling in his native France and in Canada. By 1972, he had come to the United States and was the biggest draw in the wrestling world—except, perhaps, for Hulk Hogan.

Hogan held championships for years and fought many other wrestling **legends**, including "Rowdy" Roddy Piper and Ultimate Warrior. But he also starred in movies, had his own cartoon on TV, and was even on *Saturday Night Live*! His incredible popularity in the 1980s and 1990s was known as Hulkamania.

ANDRE THE GIANT VS. "ROWDY" RODDY PIPER

HULK HOGAN OFTEN CALLED HIS ARMS "24-INCH PYTHONS," REFERRING TO HOW BIG THEY WERE AROUND. THIS WAS LIKELY EXAGGERATED, AS SIZE OFTEN IS IN PRO WRESTLING.

THE UNSTOPPABLE FORCE VS. THE IMMOVABLE OBJECT

IN 1987, ANDRE WAS BELOVED BY FANS AND HAD BEEN UNDEFEATED FOR 15 YEARS. AT WRESTLEMANIA III, IN FRONT OF MORE THAN 90,000 FANS, HE FACED HULK HOGAN IN THE RING. THEY PUT ON A LEGENDARY MATCH, DESPITE THE EFFECTS A TERRIBLE BACK INJURY FROM YEARS BEFORE HAD ON ANDRE. HOGAN WON, CEMENTING HIMSELF AS THE BIGGEST STAR IN PROFESSIONAL WRESTLING.

THE HEARTBREAK KID

Being a great wrestler means performing well in the ring, connecting with the audience, and being able to cut—or say—a promo well. Shawn Michaels did all that, but he also had the "it" factor that takes wrestlers from great to the best. Shawn's **charisma** helped carry him through more than 20 years in the ring as a member of tag team The Rockers and popular **stables** DX and the Kliq.

Shawn Michaels was in the first WWE ladder match in 1992 and the first Elimination Chamber match. He headlined WrestleMania. In 2016, *Sports Illustrated* named him the second-greatest wrestler of all time, after Ric Flair.

SHAWN MICHAELS, SOMETIMES CALLED THE HEARTBREAK KID OR HBK, USED A FINISHING MOVE CALLED "SWEET CHIN MUSIC"—A KICK TO THE FACE OF HIS OPPONENT.

TAKING ON TAKER

SHAWN MICHAELS FACED ANOTHER PRO WRESTLING GREAT MANY TIMES: THE UNDERTAKER. THEIR MATCH AT WRESTLEMANIA 25 IN 2009 IS OFTEN SAID TO BE THE BEST MATCH OF ALL TIME. SHAWN LATER SAID: "THERE AREN'T MANY TIMES I'VE COME OUT OF THE RING WHEN I HAVEN'T FELT LIKE...I COULD HAVE DONE SOMETHING BETTER...BUT THAT MATCH...THAT'S ONE THAT I DON'T KNOW I CAN SAY THAT WITH."

THAT'S THE BOTTOM LINE!

During the late 1990s and early 2000s, pro wrestling was at a peak of popularity. No small part of that was due to "Stone Cold" Steve Austin, the **embodiment** of a time now known as the Attitude Era.

Stone Cold not only had a finishing move that seemed to strike out of nowhere—the Stone Cold Stunner—but also delivered promos with such believability and passion, fans couldn't help but root for him, even when he was a heel. He also feuded throughout his career with the very biggest name in the wrestling industry: Vince McMahon, owner of the WWF (now WWE).

MONDAY NIGHT WARS

FROM 1995 TO 2001, WORLD CHAMPIONSHIP WRESTLING (WCW) AND THE WWF COMPETED AGAINST ONE ANOTHER, EACH AIRING A SHOW ON MONDAY NIGHTS. STONE COLD'S POPULARITY AT THE TIME HELPED THE WWF EVENTUALLY WIN THE WAR FOR VIEWERS. THEN, THE OWNER OF THE WWF BOUGHT WCW AND COMBINED THE COMPANIES INTO WHAT WOULD BECOME THE WWE.

THE PEOPLE'S CHAMPION

No modern professional wrestler has yet to become a bigger star outside of pro wrestling than Dwayne "The Rock" Johnson. His success as an actor today comes partly from his years delivering his catchphrases in the ring, telling opponents to "know your role and shut your mouth" and asking if they "smell what The Rock is cooking."

The Rock was charismatic and earned his place as one of the best when he was able to create his overconfident character both on the mic and in the ring. He was such a big draw that he would be in the main event at WrestleMania 3 years in a row, from 1999 to 2001.

PART OF A LEGACY

IT'S NO ACCIDENT THE ROCK IS GREAT IN THE RING. IT'S IN HIS BLOOD! BOTH HIS FATHER, ROCKY JOHNSON, AND GRANDFATHER, PETER MAIVIA, ARE IN THE WWE HALL OF FAME. OTHER FAMILY MEMBERS OF HIS COMPETE IN THE WWE TODAY: ROMAN REIGNS, THE USOS, AND NIA JAX.

HUSTLE, LOYALTY, RESPECT

It's impossible to go to a professional wrestling show and not see someone wearing a John Cena T-shirt or headband. Cena was the "it guy" of the WWE for many of the almost 20 years he has spent with the company. He has performed as the main event at WrestleMania five times, feuded with the biggest names, and held world championships 16 times.

Cena may not have the most **diverse** set of moves in the ring, but he's known for working hard and coming back from injuries better and stronger than ever.

CENA AND THE ROCK FOUGHT EACH OTHER AS THE MAIN EVENT OF WRESTLEMANIA IN 2012 AND 2013.

CENA AND MAKE-A-WISH

CENA IS ONE OF THE MOST SUCCESSFUL PRO WRESTLERS OF ALL TIME, AND HE'S USED THAT SUCCESS FOR MORE THAN MAKING MONEY. CENA HAS GRANTED NEARLY 600 WISHES FOR CHILDREN SUFFERING WITH TERRIBLE ILLNESSES THROUGH THE MAKE-A-WISH FOUNDATION. THAT'S MORE THAN ANY OTHER CELEBRITY.

INTERNATIONAL GREATS

A list of pro wrestling greats wouldn't be complete without acknowledging international wrestlers. Mexican luchadores, or professional wrestlers, like Rey Mysterio, have brought high-flying moves and a mystery from behind their iconic masks.

Antonio Inoki is often called the best Japanese wrestler of all time. But that title might also go to Ultimo Dragon, who once held eight championship titles at once!

Canada has produced a number of great wrestlers too. In fact, Bret Hart called himself "the best there is, the best there was, and the best there ever will be." And many fans agree with him!

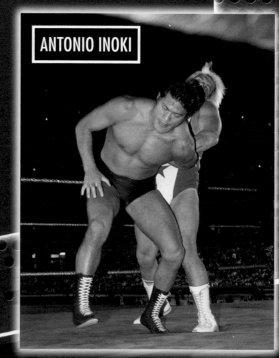

ANTONIO INOKI

WORLDWIDE TALENT

BECAUSE JAPAN AND MEXICO ARE SO WELL KNOWN FOR GREAT PRO WRESTLING, MANY OF TODAY'S STARS HAVE TRAINED AND PERFORMED IN THESE COUNTRIES. MODERN GREATS LIKE CHRIS JERICHO, AJ STYLES, AND KENNY OMEGA ALL WORKED FOR NEW JAPAN PRO WRESTLING, A BIG PRO WRESTLING COMPANY IN JAPAN.

THE FUTURE IS FEMALE

On April 7, 2019, three women made pro wrestling history. Superstars Becky Lynch, Ronda Rousey, and Charlotte Flair competed in the first women's match ever featured as the main event of WrestleMania. Only three could have this honor, but it came after many years of other women in the wrestling industry fighting to show they could be just as athletic and charismatic as the men.

Drawing from the strength and style of female wrestlers of the past, like Mae Young and Alundra Blaze, and more recent women wrestlers like the Bella Twins and Lita, the greatest female pro wrestlers are still being made today.

SASHA BANKS VS. BAYLEY

CHARLOTTE FLAIR (IN RED) IS THE DAUGHTER OF RIC FLAIR. SHE'S INCREDIBLY STRONG AND ABLE TO DO SOME OF THE BEST HIGH-FLYING MOVES IN THE WWE.

BEST WOMEN'S MATCH EVER?

IN AUGUST 2015, NXT WRESTLERS BAYLEY AND SASHA BANKS PUT ON WHAT IS OFTEN CALLED THE BEST WOMEN'S WRESTLING MATCH OF ALL TIME. BAYLEY, THE UNDERDOG IN THE MATCH, DEFEATED SASHA BANKS FOR THE NXT WOMEN'S CHAMPIONSHIP IN FRONT OF A SOLD-OUT CROWD OF 15,000 IN BROOKLYN, NEW YORK. AT THE TIME, BLEACHER REPORT SAID THE MATCH WAS "THE **EPITOME** OF WRESTLING DONE RIGHT."

GLOSSARY

charisma: a special charm that causes people to feel excited about someone

debut: a first appearance

diverse: differing from each other

dominate: to be the best, have the best position, or have control

embodiment: the representation in human form

epitome: a perfect example

legend: someone known for doing something very well

massive: very large

opponent: the person or team you must beat to win a game

predetermine: to decide beforehand

retire: to leave a job

signature: something that is especially connected with someone

Soviet Union: a former communist country that stretched from eastern Europe to Asia and was also known as the USSR

stable: in pro wrestling, a group that often performs and competes together

submit: allowing an opponent to win

technique: the way of doing a skill or ability to perform a job

FOR MORE INFORMATION

BOOKS

Rebman, Nick. *Wrestling.* Lake Elmo, MN: Focus Readers, 2019.

Santos, Rita. *Dwayne "The Rock" Johnson: Pro Wrestler and Actor.* New York, NY: Enslow Publishing, 2020.

Sherman, Jill. *Ronda Rousey.* Mankato, MN: Amicus/Amicus Ink, 2020.

WEBSITES

WWE
www.wwe.com
Stay up to date on your favorite pro wrestlers through the official website of World Wrestling Entertainment.

Wrestling USA Magazine
www.wrestlingusa.com
Find out the latest news in NCAA wrestling and learn more about the sport on this site.

INDEX